National Parks
Yellowstone

AUDRA WALLACE

Children's Press®
An Imprint of Scholastic Inc.

Content Consultant
James Gramann, PhD
Professor, Department of Recreation, Park and Tourism Sciences
Texas A&M University, College Station, Texas

Library of Congress Cataloging-in-Publication Data

Names: Wallace, Audra, author.
Title: Yellowstone / by Audra Wallace.
Description: New York, NY : Children's Press, an imprint of Scholastic Inc.,
    2018. | Series: A true book | Includes bibliographical references and index.
Identifiers: LCCN 2016051663 | ISBN 9780531233962 (library binding : alkaline
    paper) | ISBN 9780531240236 (paperback : alkaline paper)
Subjects: LCSH: Yellowstone National Park—Juvenile literature.
Classification: LCC F722 .W34 2018 | DDC 978.7/52—dc23
LC record available at https://lccn.loc.gov/2016051663

All rights reserved. Published in 2018 by Children's Press, an imprint of Scholastic Inc.
Printed in China 62

SCHOLASTIC, CHILDREN'S PRESS, A TRUE BOOK™, and associated logos are trademarks and/or registered trademarks of Scholastic Inc., 557 Broadway, New York, NY 10012.
1 2 3 4 5 6 7 8 9 10 R 27 26 25 24 23 22 21 20 19 18

Front cover: Old Faithful geyser
Front cover (inset): Bison
Back cover: Grand Prismatic Spring

Find the Truth!

Everything you are about to read is true *except* for one of the sentences on this page.

Which one is **TRUE**?

T or F   Miners were the first people to discover Yellowstone.

T or F   Yellowstone National Park is an active volcano.

Find the answers in this book.

Contents

THE BIG TRUTH!

National Parks Field Guide: Yellowstone

A grizzly bear

A deer among aspen trees

A hiker

CHAPTER 1

A Long History

Imagine a place where water spouts hundreds of feet into the air. Boiling pools of mud bubble and burst. That place is real! It's called Yellowstone National Park. Yellowstone is located in Wyoming and parts of Idaho and Montana. The park is famous for its more than 10,000 active **hydrothermal** features, such as **geysers** and mudpots. These hot spots helped inspire people to make Yellowstone the first national park in the United States.

Yellowstone is home to the largest bison population on U.S. public land.

Yellowstone National Park

Lots of Lava

Millions of years ago, volcanoes helped form Yellowstone. **Magma** from deep inside Earth erupted through the ground. Huge amounts of lava flowed out. When the lava cooled, it hardened into rock. Over time, the rocks built up into mountains. Believe it or not, red-hot magma still boils right below the park's surface. In fact, Yellowstone sits inside three overlapping **calderas**. Luckily, there hasn't been an eruption for more than 640,000 years!

A Timeline About Traveling to Yellowstone

11,000 years ago
Native Americans first travel through Yellowstone on foot.

1700s
Native groups in the region begin traveling on horseback.

1877
The first wagons make their way through Yellowstone.

People in Yellowstone

Native Americans discovered Yellowstone thousands of years ago. Groups such as the Siksika, Bannocks, Absaroka, and Shoshone once followed **migrating** wildlife through the area. They hunted bison, elk, and bighorn sheep. **Archaeologists** have found arrowheads and other tools that date back about 11,000 years. Native Americans carved the arrowheads from the hard, glass-like volcanic rock that makes up the park's Obsidian Cliff.

1883
The Northern Pacific Railroad brings tourists to the park for the first time.

1915
The first visitors in cars arrive in Yellowstone.

1927
Charles Lindbergh flies his plane, the *Spirit of St. Louis*, over Yellowstone.

An Unbelievable Place

The first Europeans and white Americans in Yellowstone were fur trappers. In the early 1800s, they trapped beavers for their pelts, or skins. What the trappers saw in Yellowstone amazed them. Many shared their experiences. But few people believed them. In 1869, other explorers visited Yellowstone. They made maps. Later expeditions took photographs.

Miners soon headed to Yellowstone to look for gold and other minerals. Loggers looked to its forests as a source of wood. Some people wanted to hunt there. Others feared such activities would destroy Yellowstone. They persuaded the U.S. government to protect it. On March 1, 1872, Yellowstone became the country's first national park.

Beavers were highly valued for their pelts.

National Park Fact File

A national park is land that is protected by the federal government. It is a place of importance to the United States because of its beauty, history, or value to scientists. The U.S. Congress creates a national park by passing a law. Here are some key facts about Yellowstone National Park.

Yellowstone National Park	
Location	Wyoming, Idaho, Montana
Year established	1872
Size	3,472 square miles (8,992 sq km)
Average number of visitors each year	3.4 million
Famous Features	Hydrothermal features, including geysers, hot springs, and mudpots
Tallest active geyser (in the park and the world)	Steamboat Geyser, sometimes reaching more than 300 feet (91 m)

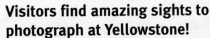

Visitors find amazing sights to photograph at Yellowstone!

Sizzling Sights

The heat that flows beneath Yellowstone has shaped the park into the popular place it is today. Millions of people visit every year to see the bubbling, steaming, bursting, and sometimes stinking features that make the park famous. From the quiet beauty of a hot spring to the sudden *whoosh* of a geyser, Yellowstone National Park has it all.

Steamboat Geyser eruptions can last as long as 40 minutes.

Superheated Springs

Thousands of hot springs bubble and boil throughout Yellowstone. These steamy pools form when water from rain and snow seeps underground. The magma beneath the park heats the water. Once heated, the water rises back to the surface through cracks in the ground. The largest hot spring in Yellowstone is Grand Prismatic Spring. It is bigger than a football field!

Different kinds of bacteria live in Grand Prismatic Spring. These tiny living things lend the water its vibrant colors.

Water flows over the step-like rock formations at Minerva Terrace.

The Mammoth Hot Springs area features numerous pools of water. The water here trickles through tiny holes in underground limestone. It carries minerals from the limestone to the surface. When the water comes into contact with the air, it produces a mineral called travertine. The travertine hardens into rock and builds up around the pools. This creates multicolored layers that look like terraces, or series of steps.

A burst from Old Faithful can last up to five minutes.

In the late 1800s, Old Faithful was used like a washing machine. Soldiers put their dirty clothes in it. The geyser shot the clothes back out. The clothes were clean!

Gushing Geysers

A geyser is a type of hot spring. But at times the water in a geyser bursts into the sky like a fountain! There are about 500 active geysers in the park. This is more than any other place on Earth! The most famous geyser is Old Faithful. It spouts water about every 60 to 100 minutes. That is how the geyser got its name. The word *faithful* describes someone or something you can depend on.

What's That Smell?

If you ever visit Yellowstone, you may see people holding their noses. Why? Some parts of the park smell like rotten eggs! The smell comes from pools of very hot water called mudpots. A gas called sulfur makes the water stink. Acid in the water turns surrounding rock into mud, making the water brown and goopy.

Some mudpots have been known to shoot hot mud up to 15 feet (4.6 meters) in the air.

Big Blasts

Along the hillsides, visitors can expect to hear the hissing and whistling of **fumaroles**. These holes in the ground release scorching steam and other gases into the air. Fumaroles are the hottest hydrothermal features in the park. The temperature of the water **vapor** escaping from them can reach up to 280 degrees Fahrenheit (138 degrees Celsius).

Don't get too close to fumaroles. The vapor that comes out of them is extremely hot.

Volcano Alert!

Yellowstone is one big, active volcano. If the volcano were to erupt, it would pose a serious danger to the surrounding area. Its blast could even cover much of the United States and Canada with ash. But don't worry! Scientists at the Yellowstone Volcano Observatory do not think an eruption will happen anytime in the near future. They monitor the park for signs of volcanic activity. If they were to detect a big eruption coming, they would warn people to leave the area.

If you see a black bear cub like this one, stay alert! Its mother is almost certainly nearby.

CHAPTER 3

Creature Comebacks

Yellowstone is home to towering mountains, deep forests, and vast valleys. But these places are more than just beautiful to look at. They provide habitats for more than 300 different species of animals. The most famous are bison, gray wolves, and grizzly bears. All three were once in danger of dying out. But they have all made big comebacks in the park.

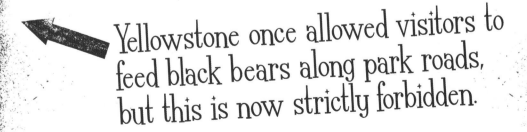

Yellowstone once allowed visitors to feed black bears along park roads, but this is now strictly forbidden.

Bison Boom

Bison are the easiest animals to spot. These shaggy beasts are the biggest land animals in North America. For hundreds of years, many Native Americans depended on bison for food and clothing. Later, American settlers hunted bison in huge numbers. By 1900, bison had almost died out. A few survived in Yellowstone. The park prohibited any more hunting. Over time, the bison population grew. More than 5,000 bison now graze in Yellowstone's meadows and grasslands.

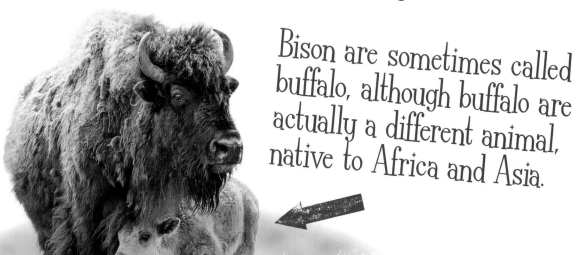

Bison are sometimes called buffalo, although buffalo are actually a different animal, native to Africa and Asia.

A Howling Return

Gray wolves are important to Yellowstone's ecosystem. They prowl the park for elk. Long ago, people killed all the wolves in Yellowstone. But without wolves as predators, the elk population grew out of control. The elk ate huge amounts of young plants, leaving other animals little to eat. In 1995, wolves were brought back to Yellowstone. Now, they help control elk numbers. They also keep the elk moving. Herds don't stay in one place for long for fear of being hunted. This prevents overgrazing and allows young plants to flourish.

About 600 gray wolves live in and around the park.

Good News for Grizzlies

Alongside the more common black bears, grizzly bears now roam Yellowstone's forests and valleys. They were once found across the United States. Today, the park is one of the few places where wild grizzlies can still be found. About 700 of them live in and around Yellowstone. They gobble up berries and catch fish in the park's rivers. But when spring comes, bison and elk beware! Grizzly bears hunt them for dinner.

In 1975, only about 130 grizzly bears lived in Yellowstone.

A sign marks an area where people could once see bears eating.

Don't Feed the Bears!

In the early 1900s, there were no garbage trucks to haul trash away from the park. Garbage was dumped in piles outside. These trash heaps attracted bears. The park set up bleachers nearby so tourists could see bears up close. But bears soon began seeking out human food elsewhere. Some learned to beg for food along park roads. That put people in danger. Today, garbage is hauled away, and people must keep food in bear-proof bins.

National Parks Field Guide:
Yellowstone

Here are a few of the hundreds of fascinating animals you may see in the park.

Bald eagle

Scientific name: *Haliaeetus leucocephalus*

Habitat: Near lakes and rivers; nests can be found in trees by the water

Diet: Mostly fish

Fact: The bald eagle is the national symbol of the United States.

Blotched tiger salamander

Scientific name: *Ambystoma tigrinum melanostictum*

Habitat: Throughout park; it breeds in ponds and lakes without fish

Diet: Insects, frogs, and other small animals

Fact: This salamander can grow up to 9 inches (23 centimeters) long.

Elk

Scientific name: *Cervus canadensis*

Habitat: Grasslands in high elevations in summer; generally move to lower elevations and river valleys in winter

Diet: Grass, plants, leaves

Fact: There are up to 20,000 elk in Yellowstone during the summer.

Mountain lion

Scientific name: *Puma concolor*

Habitat: Rugged areas with plenty of prey

Diet: Elk, mule deer, and marmots and other small mammals

Fact: Mountain lions, also known as cougars, panthers, pumas, and catamounts, are one of the largest cats in North America.

Sagebrush lizard

Scientific name: *Sceloporus graciosus*

Habitat: Dry, rocky areas and geyser basins

Diet: Insects and spiders

Fact: This spiny reptile is the only lizard in Yellowstone.

Yellowstone cutthroat trout

Scientific name: *Oncorhynchus clarkii bouvieri*

Habitat: Streams and lakes with cold, clear water

Diet: Mostly aquatic insects like mayflies, stoneflies, and caddisflies

Fact: An important food source for many birds and mammals, these fish are only found in Yellowstone!

Plenty of Plants

More than 1,000 plants grow in Yellowstone. Most of the trees are conifers. These evergreen trees are built to survive Yellowstone's frigid winters, when temperatures drop well below freezing. A few **deciduous** trees brighten up the landscape when their leaves change color in the fall. In the spring and summer, hundreds of wildflowers blossom throughout the park.

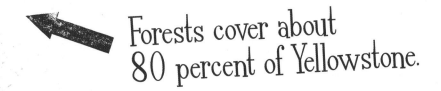

Forests cover about 80 percent of Yellowstone.

Lodgepole pines can live for up to 400 years.

Built to Last

Lodgepole pines are pretty much everywhere in Yellowstone. They make up more than 80 percent of the forests. Native Americans once used these tall, thin trees to build tepees or wickiups. Douglas fir trees grow in places such as Lamar and Hayden Valley. Their thick bark protects them from wildfires that occasionally threaten the forests. Other conifers, including Engelmann spruce and Rocky Mountain juniper, are found in the park, too.

Trembling Trees

The most common deciduous tree in Yellowstone is the quaking aspen. Its thin leaves inspired the tree's name. They flutter in the slightest breeze. When autumn arrives, the leaves change from green to a bright yellow. Animals like deer and beavers feast on the fallen leaves. Groves of cottonwood and willow trees also grow in parts of the park.

Can you spot the deer camouflaged among the aspen trees?

Beautiful Blossoms

As the weather warms, wildflowers fill the Yellowstone landscape with a rainbow of colors. Many of them can be seen in the meadows. Common wildflowers include arnica, bluebells, Indian paintbrush, shooting stars, and lupines. But visitors to the park should not pick them. Many animals eat the seeds, berries, and petals of wildflowers. Bees and other insects depend on the **nectar** and pollen from the blossoms to survive.

The Indian paintbrush is Wyoming's state flower.

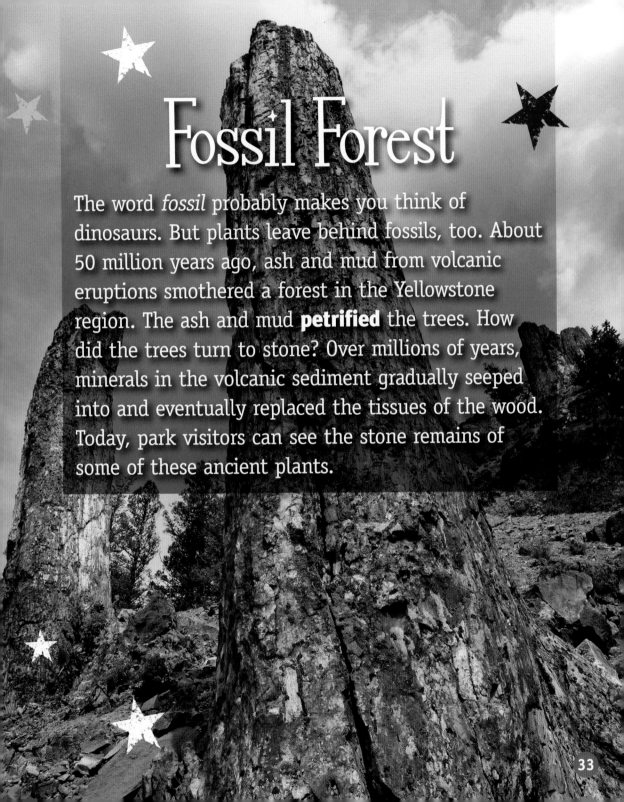

Fossil Forest

The word *fossil* probably makes you think of dinosaurs. But plants leave behind fossils, too. About 50 million years ago, ash and mud from volcanic eruptions smothered a forest in the Yellowstone region. The ash and mud **petrified** the trees. How did the trees turn to stone? Over millions of years, minerals in the volcanic sediment gradually seeped into and eventually replaced the tissues of the wood. Today, park visitors can see the stone remains of some of these ancient plants.

At Yellowstone, a bear sighting can happen just about anywhere!

CHAPTER 5

Preserving the Park

Yellowstone has come a long way since it became the United States' first national park. In the beginning, it was more like an amusement park. Wild animals were caged and put on display to entertain tourists. Laundry areas were set up near geysers and hot springs. People bathed in the pools at Mammoth Hot Springs. Nowadays, the park works hard to balance the visitor experience with caring for Yellowstone's natural resources.

About 150 inches (381 cm) of snow falls in Yellowstone each year.

Park Protectors

The park is one of the last **temperate** ecosystems on Earth that hasn't been drastically changed by people. The National Park Service wants to keep the park in good condition. Park rangers play a big role in protecting Yellowstone's natural resources and its more than 1,800 known archaeological sites. They teach visitors about Yellowstone's history and enforce safety rules. They also support efforts that protect the land, animals, and plants.

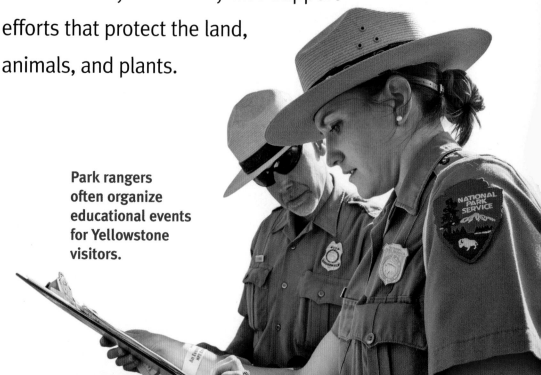

Park rangers often organize educational events for Yellowstone visitors.

A geologist collects samples of bacteria near the Grand Prismatic Spring.

Scientists have an important job in the park, too. They study the park's weather and thermal features, as well as its many species and habitats. One concern they have is that Yellowstone's climate is changing. Average temperatures in the park are higher now than they were 50 years ago. There are also about 30 fewer days per year with snow on the ground. Scientists plan to keep a close eye on how these changes affect life in Yellowstone.

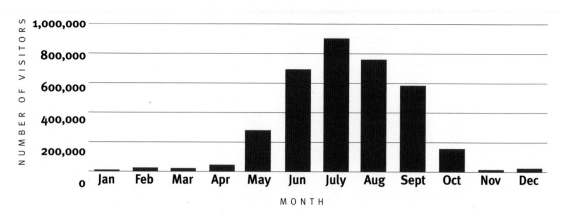

Average Monthly Visitation (1979-2015)

NUMBER OF VISITORS

| | 1,000,000 |
| 800,000 |
| 600,000 |
| 400,000 |
| 200,000 |
| 0 | Jan Feb Mar Apr May Jun July Aug Sept Oct Nov Dec |

MONTH

A Popular Park

More than three million people from around the world visit Yellowstone each year, and that number is growing fast. This may seem like good news. However, too many tourists can put a strain on the park's facilities, trails, and roads. Traffic is already a big problem, especially when wild animals are crossing the road. They cause what is known as "wildlife jams."

Huge crowds often gather at popular landmarks such as Old Faithful.

The National Park Service works to make sure Yellowstone continues to be a park that people can enjoy for years to come. Projects such as recycling programs, road repairs, and new educational centers are helping achieve that goal. They want everyone to have the chance to see Yellowstone as it has always been: a natural wonder and a national treasure. ★

An erupting geyser provides a memorable photo opportunity.

Map Mystery

The highest peak in Yellowstone is 11,372 feet (3,466 meters) tall. What is its name? Follow the directions below to find the answer.

Directions

1. Start at the Roosevelt Arch by the north entrance of the park.

2. Go south to Old Faithful.

3. Travel east across Yellowstone Lake to Frank Island.

4. You're almost there! Head southeast.

5. Find the mountain that shares its name with a bird and you will solve the mystery.

YELLOWSTONE
NATIONAL PARK

Albright Visitor Center

North Entrance

Roosevelt Arch

Mammoth Hot Springs

Northeast Entrance

Obsidian Cliff

Mount Washburn

Lamar Valley

Canyon Visitor Education Center

Grand Canyon of the Yellowstone

Lower Falls
Upper Falls

West Entrance

Artists Paintpot

Hayden Valley

Fishing Bridge Visitor Center

Fountain Paint Pot

Yellowstone Lake

East Entrance

Old Faithful

Frank Island

Old Faithful Visitor Education Center

Grant Visitor Center

Eagle Peak

South Entrance

Compass Rose

North

West ◆ East

South

U.S.

Area of map

Alaska and Hawai'i are not drawn to scale or placed in their proper places.

Be an Animal Tracker!

If you're ever in Yellowstone, keep an eye out for these animal tracks. They'll help you know which animals are in the area.

Bighorn sheep
Hoof length: 3 inches (8 cm)

Bison
Hoof length: 5 inches (13 cm)

Elk

Hoof length: 3 inches (8 cm)

Gray wolf

Paw length: 5 inches (13 cm)

Grizzly bear

Paw length: 6 inches (15 cm)

Mountain lion

Paw length: 3 inches (8 cm)

True Statistics

Annual number of earthquakes per year: 1,000 to 3,000

Number of active hydrothermal features: More than 10,000

Number of active geysers: About 500

Number of waterfalls more than 15 feet (4.6 m) high: At least 350

Number of bird species: About 150

Number of mammal species in the park: 67

Number of fish species: 16, including 11 native and 5 non-native

Number of amphibian species: 5

Number of reptile species: 6

Did you find the truth?

(F) Miners were the first people to discover Yellowstone.

(T) Yellowstone National Park is an active volcano.

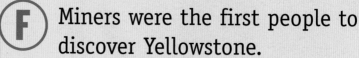

Resources

Books

Flynn, Sarah Wassner, and Julie Beer. *National Parks Guide U.S.A.* Washington, DC: National Geographic, 2016.

Frisch, Nate. *Yellowstone National Park*. Mankato, MN: Creative Paperbacks, 2014.

Nagle, Francis. *Yellowstone National Park*. New York: Gareth Stevens Publishing, 2015.

Visit this Scholastic website for more information on Yellowstone National Park:
★ www.factsfornow.scholastic.com
Enter the keyword **Yellowstone**

Important Words

archaeologists (ahr-kee-AH-luh-jists) people who study the distant past by digging up and examining its physical remains, such as old buildings, household objects, and bones

calderas (kal-DARE-uhz) huge craters located at the sites of powerful volcanic eruptions

deciduous (di-SIJ-oo-uhs) shedding all leaves every year in the fall

fumaroles (FYOOM-uh-rolz) vents through which volcanic gases escape

geysers (GYE-zurz) underground hot springs that shoot boiling water and steam into the air

hydrothermal (hye-druh-THUR-muhl) having to do with the action of heated water in the earth's crust

magma (MAG-muh) melted rock found beneath the earth's surface; when it reaches the surface, it's called lava

migrating (MYE-grate-ing) moving to another area or climate at a particular time of year

nectar (NEK-tur) a sweet liquid from flowers that bees gather and make into honey

petrified (PET-ruh-fide) changed to become hard like stone because minerals have seeped into its cells

temperate (TEM-pur-it) an area that has neither very high nor very low temperatures

vapor (VAY-pur) a gas formed from something that is usually a liquid or solid at normal temperatures

Index

Page numbers in **bold** indicate illustrations.

About the Author

Audra Wallace graduated from Ithaca College, where she studied film production and elementary education. Her passion for writing nonfiction and teaching kids led her to a position with Scholastic. Since 2006, Wallace has written and edited the award-winning classroom magazine *Scholastic News* Edition 3. She and her family enjoy exploring the great outdoors near their home in New York—and beyond!